## CANADA
## IN A CHANGING WORLD ECONOMY

The echoes of Laurier's remark about Canada and the twentieth century are taking a long time to fade away. It is one of the purposes of Professor Johnson's Alan B. Flaunt Lectures (given at Carleton University in 1962) to silence them, for they can prove dangerous and misleading—like a siren song—in the formulation of Canadian economic policy at this time. The success of the Common Market, Britain's request for membership, President Kennedy's desire for tariff flexibility and reductions in the United States, and the recent stagnation in the North American economy (accentuated in Canada by an emphasis on monetary stability)—these are signs of change in the economic climate of the world. The requisite adaptations are the most important problem facing those who govern the economic life of this country, and they must be faced realistically to ensure Canada's continuing economic growth. Professor Johnson analyses his subject with his customary authoritative skill and lucidity. Written in non-technical language, this book presents an ideal summary of the contemporary economic world as it affects Canada.

HARRY G. JOHNSON was educated at Toronto, Cambridge, and Harvard universities. He has held teaching posts at Toronto, Cambridge, and Manchester, and is now Professor of Economics at the University of Chicago. He has published many papers and essays, and is the editor of the *Journal of Political Economy*.

Alan B. Plaunt Memorial Lectures
Carleton University, Ottawa, February 15, 17, 1962

# CANADA IN A CHANGING WORLD ECONOMY

*by Harry G. Johnson*

PUBLISHED
IN CO-OPERATION WITH CARLETON UNIVERSITY
BY UNIVERSITY OF TORONTO PRESS

ALAN B. PLAUNT MEMORIAL LECTURES

*Canada and Its Giant Neighbour.* By Jacob Viner (1958)

*Civil Liberties and Canadian Federalism.*
By F. R. Scott (1959)

*Roots and Values in Canadian Lives.*
By Jean-C. Falardeau (1960)

*Canada in a Changing World Economy.*
By Harry G. Johnson (1962)

Copyright, Canada, 1962, by

University of Toronto Press

Reprinted 1962, 2017

ISBN 978-1-4875-9207-3 (paper)

# CONTENTS

CANADA
IN A CHANGING WORLD ECONOMY

# 1. INTRODUCTION

WHEN THE distinguished international economist and scholar Jacob Viner was invited to inaugurate the Alan B. Plaunt Memorial Lectures four years ago, he chose to speak on the subject of Canadian-American relations. That choice, and Professor Viner's wise and scintillating lectures themselves, served brilliantly the purpose of the Plaunt Lectureships—to bring before a public audience in Canada's capital city informed discussions of great Canadian national issues. In accepting the invitation to give the Plaunt lectures this year—an invitation by which I have been both deeply honoured and strongly challenged—I have tried to serve that purpose in my turn by choosing to speak on the issue I consider to be of greatest contemporary importance to my country: the changing world economy and Canada's place in it.

Like Professor Viner before me, I approach my task with some diffidence, since as a Canadian I am sensitive to the fact that some of the things I shall have to say will be unpopular, and perhaps offensive to some members of my audience. Probably the most irritating aspects of my discourse to some of you will lie, not in any specific remarks I make, but in the implications of the general way I approach my subject. I shall place in the forefront of my argument the changing nature of the international economy, and only after I have discussed that will I turn to considering Canada's place in it specifically. This approach carries the implication that, contrary to the contentions of Mr. Bruce Hutchison and other Canadian patriots, Canada is not "a giant among nations," but in many relevant respects a small country of limited power and influence. Appreciation of this fact permeated Viner's lectures and informed most of his wise remarks; but he was able to sugar the pill by emphasizing the giant size of Canada's neighbour, whereas I shall have to dwell explicitly on Canada's limitations. While this is likely to be wounding to Canadian self-esteem, I consider it part of my duty as Plaunt Lecturer not to shrink from delivering salutary shocks of this kind. In my considered opinion one of the chief obstacles to intelligent discussion of Canadian problems, in both the political and the economic field, is the traditional tendency of Canadians to hanker after an unobtainable greatness and to seek to attain it by methods contrary to Canada's true self-interest.

To start with, I shall be concerned with describing and commenting on the changing world economy. That phrase no doubt suggests to you the dramatic and widely publicized changes in the foreign trade policies of various countries that have been announced in the past year: Britain's decision to apply for membership in the Common Market, the successful negotiation of the second stage of the Common Market, and President Kennedy's application to Congress for sweeping new powers of tariff reduction. I shall deal with these matters in due course; but they are surface reflections of more fundamental changes that have been going on, and will continue to go on, in the world economy, and I shall begin with these more fundamental changes.

## 2. THE CHANGING BALANCE OF POWER IN THE WORLD ECONOMY

BY FAR THE most fundamental economic development of recent years has been the dramatic shift in what might loosely be called the balance of power in the world economy, a shift marked especially by an increase in the relative importance of Europe in world economic affairs and a decline in the relative importance of North America, but also by some increase in the importance of the Communist bloc and of the underdeveloped countries. This shift has been associated with the relatively rapid industrial growth of Europe, Japan, and the Communist bloc, as compared with North America, and with the beginnings of industrialization in the underdeveloped countries. The shift, I need not point out, has been paralleled by a shift in the balance of world political power away from North America.

I have used the term "North America" to include both Canada and the United States, not merely because the shift of economic power to which I am referring has affected them both, but also because in the postwar period it has increasingly made sense to think of the economies of the two countries as one closely integrated and highly industrialized economic region.

The two North American economies emerged from the war as the one industrial region that had not been damaged, and indeed had been greatly strengthened, during the war. Partly for that reason, the region enjoyed a prolonged growth boom in the dozen or so years after the war. Canadian participation in this boom was largely based on the development and exploitation of Canadian resources for the growing United States market, the prosperity of Canada's staple export industries supporting her industrial development; and the joint processes of American investment in Canadian resource industries and manufacturing and of Canadian export to the American market linked the Canadian economy—and Canadian prosperity—ever more closely to the American economy. The combination of prosperity and growing interdependence with the United States was a new historical experience for Canada, and raised the question of "Canadian independence" in a new and acute form. In the past, Canada had been able to pursue the political goal of independence and the economic goal of prosperous economic development simultaneously, because prosperity and development depended on the growth of exports to European—primarily British—markets, and could be financed by British sources. Thus development in the past had meant increasing economic independence of the United States, whereas in the postwar period it meant increasing interdependence with the United States. In short, for the first time there appeared to be a serious conflict between the economic and political goals of the Canadian nation—and whether this was or is a real conflict is a question to which I shall return. For the moment, let me merely note that the more rapid growth of Canada than of the United States, together with the rapid expansion of Canadian secondary manufacturing in this period, also fostered the hope that Canada was shedding its dependence for growth on exporting extractive industry products and becoming capable of self-generating industrial growth.

For its part, the United States was impelled by its industrial predominance and the outbreak of the cold war to commit a growing quantity of resources from its growing national income to finance the responsibilities it assumed as undisputed leader of the non-communist world—first for the Marshall Plan and military aid, then for economic aid to underdeveloped countries. The United States also took the lead in the negotiation of mutual reduction of barriers to international trade through the General Agreement on Tariffs and Trade. In addition, without the United States consciously planning or intending it, the dollar gradually became an international reserve currency—a currency held by other countries in lieu of holdings of gold—and the United States assumed the responsibilities of a world banker. These commitments, as will appear later, have become an important source of difficulty for the United States in face of the changing balance of power in the world economy.

The result of the prolonged North American boom was that, five years or so ago, the United States and Canada seemed well established on the path of steady economic growth at an adequately rapid rate. (The Gordon Commission, you will recall, predicted that Canada would continue to grow at a rate more rapid than that predicted for the United States.) Since then, as we all know, the North American economic situation has changed sharply for the worse, and has remained so, at least in Canada: the growth boom has tailed off into a period of noticeably slower growth and high average unemployment. Explanations of the change differ in the weight they attach to different factors, but most economists would I believe agree that part of the explanation, for both the United States and Canada, is to be found in two factors: the growth of effective competition in manufacturing from Europe and Japan, and the tight money policies that have been followed by the central banks of the two countries. I would myself attach considerable weight to the effects of restrictive monetary policy aimed at the prevention of inflation, a policy which I think was seriously mistaken—especially in Canada, where the existence of a floating exchange rate relieved the monetary authorities of the need to worry about balance-of-payments deficits. I think that the policy was seriously mistaken, incidentally, because I think that the policy-makers both vastly exaggerated the evil consequences of a moderately rising price index and paid quite insufficient attention to the economic and social loss entailed by slow growth and unemployment.

Be that as it may, the slackening of economic activity and growth in North America has been one factor in the relative decline in the importance of the region in the world economy. A far more important factor has been the economic recovery of Continental Europe, and the sustained rapid economic growth of that region since 1950. The fact of European growth, and its implications, were for a long time disguised by the persistence of the dollar problem and the investment of European surpluses in dollar balances, and recognition of them was further postponed by the effects of the Suez invasion. But the formation of the Common Market and the emergence after 1957 of a chronic United States balance-of-payments problem have dramatically called attention to Europe's rapid growth and competitive power. I shall not try to explain this growth in terms of fundamental causes: some of my economist colleagues, looking at Western Germany, have attributed it to the virtues of free enterprise and competition; Canadian businessmen, looking at the same evidence, seem to find the explanation in the freedom of European business to form cartels unrestricted by a Trade Practices Commission; other observers, looking at France, have found the explanation in the virtues of long-range economic planning. Whatever the fundamental explanation—and I suspect that the psychology of military defeat and political impotence on the one hand, and the flexibility of skilled and intelligent people on the other, have a lot to do with it—the rapid growth of Europe has been based on the accumulation of capital and the application and development of modern technology and mass production. The same features characterize the continued rapid growth of the countries of the Communist bloc and of Japan; while the emergence of various underdeveloped countries as industrial producers also rests on the use of capital and the acquisition of technology and human skill.

On a broad interpretation of recent economic history, one can say that relative decline in the economic power of North America has been intimately associated with the spread of industrialization to other parts of the world. On the one hand, the second industrial revolution—the oil, electricity, mass-production, chemicals, and technology revolution—has spread from North America to the industrially advanced countries of Europe and Japan; on the other hand, industrial production has begun to develop in countries and regions formerly predominantly agricultural. The spread of industrialization around the world has meant both that North America has been losing its leadership over Europe, and that Europe and North America have begun to lose the virtual monopoly of industrial production they enjoyed up to the beginning of the Second World War.

These trends are certain to continue; and they have conflicting implications for the future prosperity and growth of North America. On the one hand, the spread of industrialization implies rising real incomes in the rest of the world, a factor which should contribute to the growth of real income in North America through the familiar mechanism of rising demand for North American products. On the other hand, the spread of industrialization implies increasing foreign competition with North American industry, and the possibility of a relative (not necessarily an absolute) decline in American living standards—a narrowing or closure of the gap between incomes per head here and in the rest of the world. In economic jargon, industrialization elsewhere has both an income and a substitution effect on foreign demand for North American products.

Before I continue with this part of the argument, let me digress for a moment to develop the proposition that the spread of industrialization represents the dynamic working out of the classical law of comparative costs. Economists customarily state this law in static terms, in some such formulation as this: given the opportunity to engage in international trade, a country will tend to specialize on the production of those commodities in which its natural, human, and capital resources give it a comparative advantage, and exchange them in foreign trade for commodities in which it has a comparative disadvantage; by so doing the country will maximize the income it can obtain from its resources. This formulation takes for granted not only the supply of human and natural resources, but also the supply of capital and, what is more important, the technology with which the factors of production are combined in the production process. A dynamic version of the law of comparative costs would take account of the fact that all of these "givens" can in fact be altered by investment—in capital goods and human skills on the one hand, in research on improved methods of production on the other—and that such investment will tend to occur whenever and wherever it promises to be exceptionally profitable.

The implication in the present context is that there is a natural and persistent tendency for capital and advanced technology to be applied wherever labour is cheap relative to its skill and educability, and thus to undermine the competitive position of countries enjoying a high standard of living derived from the possession of superior skills and technology; similarly, there is a tendency for technology to undermine high incomes accruing solely from monopolies of natural resources. The process, of course, works slowly and imperfectly, and is counterbalanced by the tendency of superior technology to be maintained by further technical progress. But it does work; and its workings have been reinforced in the present age by two developments: the prevalence in one form or another of governmental planning for economic growth, and the rise of the great international corporation producing and marketing on a world scale. It has two important implications for an internationally trading country, both of which have tended to be neglected in modern theorizing about international trade. The first is that a country's standard of living depends primarily on its level of technology and resources of capital and human skill, the gains from trade, and particularly changes in the gains from trade resulting from changes in other countries' commercial policies, playing a relatively very secondary role. The second implication is that continuing comparative advantage in a technologically advanced world may rest on superior capacity in developing the technology of a particular line of production, or —what is often associated with this—exploitation of the economies of large-scale production, rather than on any innate advantage of over-all resource endowment.

To return to the question of the effects of the spread of industrialization in the world economy on the future prosperity and growth of the North American economy, it is I think obvious from what I have just said about the dynamics of comparative costs that these effects will depend very much on how effectively the North American economy is able to adjust to the competition resulting from the application of capital and advanced technology in other countries by progressively raising the quality of its own technology and human skills and shifting from industries in which it is losing comparative advantage to those in which it is acquiring new comparative advantage. A large part of the answer depends on the flexibility and resiliency of the private enterprise system itself, a matter about which one may I think entertain a fair degree of confidence; but much of it depends on the wisdom of governmental policy, and especially on how far governmental policy facilitates or hinders the functioning of the free enterprise system—a matter about which recent experience gives much less ground for confidence. I shall return to these matters later.

## 3. THE CHANGING INTERNATIONAL ECONOMIC SYSTEM

LET ME NOW turn from the underlying change that has been going on in the world economy to its more immediate manifestations in the evolution of international economic relations and institutional arrangements. To begin with, it is useful to gain perspective by recalling the chief features of the international economic system that wartime planning for postwar reconstruction sought to establish for the postwar world. Postwar reconstruction planning was strongly influenced by the breakdown of the interwar gold exchange standard in the 1930's under the impact of international short-term capital flights ("hot money" movements), and the resulting constriction and disorganization of international trade by competitive currency depreciation, quota and exchange control restriction of imports, and bilateral trading; it was also strongly influenced by certain American prejudices in favour of conservative banking practices and the principle of non-discrimination in international trade. The reconstruction planners sought to establish an institutional framework for a multilateral non-discriminatory trading system that would secure the advantages of the gold exchange standard system of fixed exchange rates without its rigidity and vulnerability to short-term capital movements. The framework was to be embodied in three new international institutions, two of which were actually established and the third of which has been provided by a less formal substitute. The first was the International Monetary Fund, whose purpose was to provide a stronger international monetary system by providing a pool of international reserves on which members could draw to supplement their gold reserves, by accepting the right of members to control short-term capital movements, by establishing a mechanism by which members could alter their exchange rates in case of "fundamental disequilibrium," and by adopting a "scarce currency clause" by which persistent creditor countries could be disciplined. The second institution was the International Bank for Reconstruction and Development, whose purpose was to provide a flow of internationally guaranteed loans to countries in need of capital. The third, whose function was assumed by the General Agreement on Tariffs and Trade (GATT), was to embody and police a code of fair trade restriction practices, non-discrimination being the fundamental principle, and to provide an agency for the negotiation of non-discriminatory tariff reductions; but while new preferential trading arrangements were excluded, exception was made for completely discriminatory trade arrangements in the form of customs unions and free trade areas.

It is an ironical reflection on the powers of official foresight, as well as a vindication of the analytical ability of some of the contemporary critics of these arrangements, that while these institutions can justly be said to have performed useful functions in postwar economic affairs, the limitations of the principles on which they were constructed can equally be held to blame for the strains that have developed in the non-communist world economy in the past few years, and particularly for the difficulties now facing the United States. The preservation of the monetary role of gold inherent in the structure of the Fund, the development of the use of the dollar as a reserve currency prompted by the limited resources of the Fund, and the increasing unwillingness of members to contemplate changes in their par values, have brought the world back to something very like the interwar gold exchange standard; and the fact that it has proved impossible to control short-term capital flights and impolitic to discipline creditors has meant that the new gold exchange standard is as vulnerable as the old to hot money movements, and like the old has had to rely increasingly on the willingness of central banks receiving hot money—or their governments—to lend it back to the country losing it. The conservative principles of the International Bank have made it, quite appropriately, an unsuitable instrument for raising and administering the vast sums of money it is now thought obligatory for the advanced nations to contribute to the development of the backward nations, so that this burden has increasingly been assumed by the United States government. Finally, the exception of customs unions and free trade areas from the general principle of non-discrimination has legitimized the formation of the European Common Market and other projected customs unions and the resulting prospective division of the world economy into regional trading blocs, quite contrary to the intentions of the GATT system; moreover, the non-discrimination principle is likely to make it difficult for the United States to persuade the Common Market to negotiate mutual reduction of tariffs.

These reflections, however, take me to the end of a story I have yet to tell: the story of why the postwar international economic system has turned out so differently from what was expected, and particularly of why the non-communist world economy is in process of being divided between two rival giant protected trading areas, Europe and the United States. The key developments leading up to the present situation have been on the one hand the emergence after the war of the United States as the pre-eminent leader of the free world, and its assumption of the corresponding economic responsibilities to the non-communist countries, and on the other hand the subsequent emergence of the European Common Market as a potentially more powerful influence on international economic relations than the United States. The primary sources of both developments are to be found in the economic and political developments of the immediate postwar period: economically, in the unexpected difficulty and protracted delay in the restoration of the European countries to full currency convertibility and in the focusing of Europe's difficulties on a shortage of dollars; politically, in the outbreak of the cold war.

Europe's dollar problem prompted the United States

to the boldly imaginative suggestion of the Marshall Plan; the outbreak of the cold war provided a political motivation for the commitment of American resources to the support of European reconstruction, and thereafter the motivation for increasing commitment of American resources to military and economic assistance to the underdeveloped countries. The dominance of the United States in world trade, and its increasingly large foreign lending and transfer operations, together with the inconvertibility of European currencies and the unprofitability of holding international reserves in the form of gold, led to the increasing use of dollar balances as international reserves by other countries. Finally, the United States (together with Canada) took the lead in negotiating tariff reductions through GATT. In these various ways the United States rapidly assumed the responsibilities of centre country in the world economy—supplier of capital for other countries' development, reserve currency country, practitioner of a liberal trading policy—which Britain had carried in the nineteenth century (and has struggled so onerously and unprofitably to carry in the twentieth).

## 4. THE EUROPEAN ECONOMIC COMMUNITY

TO TURN TO European developments, the Common Market is fundamentally a political creation, the economic manifestation of the ambition to build a United States of Europe or European Federation, a project that a number of influential Europeans adopted at the end of the war as the only feasible means both of containing the disastrous rivalry of France and Germany and of rebuilding the political influence of Europe in face of the dominating power of the United States and Russia. The cold war both fanned this ambition in Europe and led the United States to support it strongly as a means of building up the political stability and economic strength of Europe against the communist menace. The long period of dollar shortage and dependence on Marshall Plan aid laid the foundations for the successful achievement of European economic integration, by accustoming the European governments to collaborating in economic affairs and considering each other's economic interests; an important factor here was that the aid was initially allocated according to the individual countries' dollar requirements, and had to be redistributed among them according to over-all resource needs, the Organization for European Economic Cooperation being set up for that purpose. The OEEC, however, was primarily concerned with co-operation in the reduction of quota and exchange control barriers to trade, rather than with European economic integration in the positive sense, and the development of the Common Market took place outside it and indeed in rivalry to it.

The most important factor in the successful achievement of the Common Market was the rapid economic growth that the continental countries of Europe enjoyed after 1950, a growth that occurred in spite of (or perhaps because of) the balance-of-payments difficulties most of them continued to experience. This rapid economic growth ensured the success of their first experiment with the common market idea—the European Coal and Steel Community, formed by France, Germany,

Italy, Belgium, Luxembourg, and the Netherlands, "the Six" as they soon came to be called, in 1952—and gave the participating countries the confidence to carry the experiment forward into the formation of a comprehensive common market. It is significant, in the light of later developments, that Britain was invited to participate in the Coal and Steel Community but refused to do so.

The proposal for the formation of a Common Market among the six members of the European Coal and Steel Community was first advanced early in 1955; the Treaty which gave effect to the scheme was signed in March 1957, and the European Economic Community, as it is called, came into existence on January 1, 1959. Much happened in the intervening period, but before I describe those events I should describe the economic philosophy and central features of the Common Market, since an understanding of these is essential to both appreciation of Britain's relations with it and evaluation of possible changes in its relations with the rest of the world.

As I have mentioned, the Common Market has been motivated primarily by the desire to form a political union in Europe; this motivation is strongly stamped on the economic philosophy of the Common Market Treaty, which bears a much closer resemblance to the protectionist theories of Hamilton and List than to the free trade theories of the English classical economists. That philosophy is difficult to summarize—much of it has been written by Frenchmen, and displays the combination of rhetorical flair and logical imprecision so characteristic of the rational French mind—but it can I think be reduced to three central propositions.

The first proposition is that countries can only overcome the economic disadvantages of small national markets by eliminating trade barriers among themselves so as to create a large common market; the advantages of a large market are envisaged partly in terms of the classical gains of specialization and division of labour, but much more in terms of exploitation of the economies of large-scale production, long production runs, and up-to-date technology, and it is stressed—a point Canadians should note—that only in a large market will there be sufficient competition to ensure that the advantages of large-scale production are in fact realized and passed on to the consumer in the form of lower prices. It should also be noticed that this proposition implicitly assumes that the countries concerned are employing tariffs and trade restrictions to protect their domestic industries; and that it neglects the economic loss entailed in any diversion of purchases from non-participating to participating country producers that may follow the elimination of trade barriers among participating countries and the erection of a common tariff around the market area—what Professor Viner has labelled the loss from trade diversion.

The second proposition is that elimination of barriers to trade—tariffs, quotas, and exchange controls—is not enough: to reap the full potential advantages of a common market it is necessary to make the market genuinely a common one by eliminating distortions and inequalities in conditions of competition. This is a far-reaching proposition: it includes not only the elimination of impediments to the free movement of goods other than those imposed by governments—the elimination of discriminatory transport charges, for example—but also the elimination of impediments to the free movement of labour, capital, and enterprise within the market area, the "harmonization" of tax systems and social legislation, and the establishment of codes enforcing competition—

though Europeans are more ready than North Americans to believe that agreements between businesses may have beneficial effects for the consumer. Most of these stipulations, it may be remarked, are unnecessary according to the pure theory of international trade, though some of them have turned out on more sophisticated analysis to be quite sensible.

The third proposition is that free competition in the market between countries widely different in their social and economic characteristics or stages of economic development is likely to have adverse effects on the economic development of some of them, and particularly of the less developed countries or regions. Consequently, it is argued, a common market is feasible only between countries with common geographical, historical, social, and economic characteristics, which characteristics will enable them to understand each other's problems and cooperate in ensuring that the benefits of economic development achieved through the common market are fairly distributed among the members. This third proposition, I need hardly point out, departs most widely from the classical argument for free trade, both in its assertion that free trade benefits the more developed at the expense of the less developed—a standard protectionist argument, which is also used to justify protection of European producers against American competition—and in its emphasis on the need for close governmental collaboration among the members of the common market. The belief that free trade is unfair to the underdeveloped is of course very widely held in the modern world; in Canada it is one of the few beliefs that the Ontario manufacturer and the Maritimer have in common.

The economic philosophy I have just outlined is embodied in the Treaty of Rome. Again, I shall confine myself to describing the central points. First and foremost, the Treaty provides for the establishment of a customs union—that is, the elimination of tariffs and other restrictions on trade between members and the adoption of a common tariff schedule on their imports from non-members—to be brought into effect in three stages; the first of these has since been accelerated, and was completed early this year. Second, the Treaty provides for free movement of labour and capital and the elimination of a variety of distortions of competitive conditions; these latter provisions include the adoption of a common agricultural policy (the Europeans employ minimum prices and import restrictions to protect their agriculture) and a common transport policy. Third, the Treaty provides certain institutions to facilitate adjustment of participating countries to the Common Market, notably a European Social Fund to finance the retraining of labour and a European Investment Bank to assist the financing of investment in underdeveloped parts of the Community. Fourth, the Treaty provides a set of supranational institutions to direct the transition to and operation of the Community, of which the most important are an independent Commission to do the work, and a Council of Ministers of the member countries to take the final decisions; from the beginning of the second (present) stage of the establishment of the European Economic Community, these decisions are to be arrived at by a qualified majority vote, so that a member may be obliged to act against its own preference.

The Common Market scheme, as I have mentioned, was first proposed in 1955; its prospective fruition threatened to split the European countries, which hitherto had been co-operating in the reduction of trade barriers in the OEEC, into two rival groups. This prospect seriously alarmed the British Government, on grounds both of altruism—the threat to the restoration of a liberal world trading order—and of economic self-interest—the threat to Britain's exports to the Six. Not only did exports to the Six account for about one-eighth of Britain's total exports, but their demand for imports of manufactured goods was growing far faster than the demand of any of Britain's other markets. On the other hand, Britain did not feel that she could join the Common Market, for three main reasons: aversion to the surrender of sovereignty to supra-national institutions, and to the grander ultimate project of political unification of Europe; unwillingness to switch from her own system of protecting agriculture by subsidies to the continental system of protecting agriculture by price supports and import restrictions; and unwillingness to sacrifice Commonwealth trading relations, a consideration which bulks larger in British thinking than some Canadians seem to believe.

With characteristic ingenuity, the British government devised a scheme to resolve the dilemma: it proposed the formation of a European Free Trade Area in industrial products, in which both the Common Market countries and the other members of the OEEC would participate, and which would be administered by the regular OEEC procedures. In a free trade area, each member eliminates tariffs on imports from other members but retains control of its own tariffs; and this feature, combined with the exclusion of agriculture, would have enabled Britain to secure the free access to the European market for her manufactures that she desired, while leaving the competitive position of something like 90 per cent of Commonwealth exports to Britain unaffected.

The cleverness of this scheme and its concentration

on economics to the exclusion of political considerations were its undoing. The supporters of the European Economic Community, particularly the French, realized that the Free Trade Area would offer participants the economic benefits of free trade in industrial products without obliging them to accept the other forms of economic integration and the political commitments involved in the Common Market; they proceeded to block the scheme, first by using delaying tactics and finally by breaking off negotiations. In this strategy they relied on United States support for the idea of European integration and antipathy to the weaker Free Trade Area scheme. The British went on to negotiate a Free Trade Association with six other countries of "outer Europe," an Association which came into effect in July 1960; but even at the time this Association appeared to be more of a temporary bargaining tactic than a permanent alternative to a British accommodation with the Six, and Britain's decision to apply for membership in the Common Market, announced at the end of July 1961, has confirmed this impression.

Britain had already drifted a long way towards willingness to accept the terms of membership in the Common Market during the negotiations over the Free Trade Area. For one thing, the shock of the failure of Suez, and the Commonwealth reaction to Britain's action, had forced the British to revise drastically downwards their opinion of their own importance in world political and military affairs, and to turn their attention towards Europe rather than the Commonwealth as an area for the exercise of the British talent for leadership. For another thing, the dramatic contrast between their own slow growth rate and the rapid growth of Continental Europe fostered the hope that by associating their economy with Europe's they could accelerate economically. I would stress that this is a hope, not a valid deduction from economic theory or economic history; but it now has a powerful hold on the British imagination, as does the whole philosophy of competition in a large market. Finally, the contrast between the high rate of growth of European manufactured imports and the relatively much lower rate of growth of Commonwealth imports suggested that in foreign trade policy they were backing the wrong horse, that "the Commonwealth is a wasting asset." These ideas have continued to germinate in British public discussion, and have been stimulated by observation of the continued rapid growth of the Six and the starkly contrasting relative stagnation of Britain, a stagnation associated with the chronic weakness of the British balance of payments and the policies required to deal with it. The decision to apply for membership was obviously prompted by the 1961 balance-of-payments crisis, though it was probably also influenced by continued American pressure on Britain to join.

An application for membership in the Common Market, however, is an engagement and not a wedding. Whether Britain actually joins will depend on whether the terms she can negotiate are acceptable to British public opinion—which would probably be tested by an election—and that will depend in part on whether these terms conform to British conceptions of Britain's responsibilities to the Commonwealth—which is not exactly the same thing as conformity to the leading Commonwealth countries' conceptions of Britain's responsibilities to them. I am not prepared to venture a guess as to the probable outcome.

## 5. STRAINS ON
## THE AMERICAN DOLLAR

IN DISCUSSING the development of the Common Market, I have stressed the strong formative influence of the rapid postwar economic growth of Continental Europe. That rapid growth, and the increasingly strong competitive position of Europe in world markets associated with it, eventually permitted the restoration of full convertibility of European currencies, which was effected at the end of 1958 just prior to the initiation of the Common Market, and the virtual termination of balance-of-payments discrimination against dollar imports into Europe, effected subsequently. The achievement of these goals of postwar planning and prolonged North American endeavour has, however, been more than slightly soured by the simultaneous emergence of the Common Market as a discriminatory regional trading bloc. It has been further soured by the fact that the recovery of Europe has been accompanied by a weakening of the balance-of-payments position of the United States, which has become a chronic deficit country on a serious scale. The balance-of-payments difficulties the United States has experienced over the past four years have made the American Administration acutely aware of the burdensomeness of the responsibilities of the centre country in the world economy that the United States assumed in the immediate postwar period, and have led the United States authorities to attempt to induce the European countries to assume a larger share of these responsibilities, commensurate with Europe's growing international economic and political status; but the weakness of the United States balance-of-payments position has made it increasingly difficult for the United States to give strong leadership in making further progress towards a liberal trading world, and it is therefore doubtful whether the free world economy will evolve in that direction rather than—as at present seems more likely—in the direction of regional trading arrangements.

The balance-of-payments difficulties the United States has experienced since 1958 have had two aspects: on the one hand, the United States has had a chronic deficit, which averaged $3.7 billion a year in 1958–60; on the other it has suffered from short-term capital outflows prompted by higher interest rates in Europe or by loss of confidence in the dollar. On the surface, these difficulties can be attributed to a relative loss of American competitiveness in world markets, associated with a rise in American money costs relative to European. Fundamentally, however, they reflect the postwar evolution of the international monetary system into a rigid and potentially dangerously unstable system.

The International Monetary Fund, it will be recalled, was intended to provide a more flexible international monetary system than the interwar gold exchange standard: first, by providing for agreed changes in exchange rates in cases of "fundamental disequilibrium"; second, by enabling creditors to be disciplined by the use of the scarce currency clause; and third, by providing additional reserves and enabling countries to reduce reserve losses by controlling short-term capital movements. In fact the major countries have proved extremely unwilling to change their exchange rates, especially to appreciate them; and the scarce currency clause has never been used, for the simple reason that no one is willing to try to discipline a creditor who can be persuaded to put up more money. In consequence, the burden of correcting balance-of-payments disequilibrium has been transferred largely to the domestic policies of deficit countries. This implies a larger need for international reserves; but the postwar inflation has reduced the real value both of gold stocks and IMF resources and of the annual contribution to reserves from new gold production.

The gap has been filled by increasing use of the dollar as an international reserve currency; but the consequence of this has been a steady growth in United States short-term dollar liabilities relative to gold reserves, to the point where the former exceed the latter. This in turn has meant both an obligation on the United States to keep faith with its creditors by maintaining the gold value of the dollar, and increased difficulty in doing so because any loss of gold due to balance-of-payments deficits or interest-induced capital outflows may inspire speculation against the dollar and rapid withdrawal of deposits in the form of gold. In short, the postwar monetary system has regressed towards the interwar system, with the United States instead of Britain as reserve currency country; and while exchange rates are not quite so immutably rigid as they were under the earlier system, this is probably more than compensated by the much reduced willingness of countries to balance their international accounts by severe internal deflation.

Along with other measures it has taken to overcome its deficits, the United States has sought to persuade the European countries to assume a larger share of the responsibilities of centre country—responsibilities which, as I have explained, include the international monetary system, development aid, and trade policy. In the money field, the United States has sought for the provision of additional international reserves in the form in which experience has shown them to be needed most—additional IMF resources of the European currencies into which short-term capital is most likely to fly, resources on which the United States can draw to offset such capital flights. In this quest it has been successful: the required resources have been provided by the recently announced agreement of ten leading industrial countries (including Canada) to provide $6 billion of standby credit to the International Monetary Fund. But the details of the agreement leave some doubt as to how effective the arrangement will prove in bolstering the modern gold exchange standard, since the agreement leaves the creditors a great deal of discretion concerning the amounts of credit they will actually provide in particular cases.

In the aid and trade fields the effort to persuade Europe to share responsibilities has made no comparable visible progress. The effort has been based, ideologically, on the discovery by the United States of the "Atlantic Community" of Western Europe, the United States, and Canada—a concept originated by Mr. Lester Pearson—as the natural unit of leadership in the free world. To give effect to this concept, the United States has taken the lead in reconstituting the OEEC as the Organization for Economic Co-operation and Development, with Canada and the United States as full members, and will seek to turn the new organization into an agency for extracting more capital for the underdeveloped from Europe. The United States also evidently hopes that the "Atlantic Community" concept will help to persuade the Common Market to negotiate mutual tariff reductions.

Some success in that direction has already been achieved, with the agreement on mutual reduction of the Common Market and American tariffs in the present round of GATT negotiations, negotiations which were preceded by a conditional twenty per cent reduction of the Common Market tariff that was obviously offered in response to United States pressure. But it is extremely unlikely that the Europeans will be sufficiently impressed by the ideal of strengthening the North Atlantic Community— a concept that has a certain aroma of sucker-bait about it —to take the lead from the United States in the march towards freer trade. It is even doubtful how far they would go in negotiating mutual tariff reductions with the United States, given the political purpose and economic philosophy of the Common Market and the fact that any reductions would have to be generalized in accordance with the most-favoured-nations clause—and remembering the fate of the European Free Trade Area. It is possible, however, that the Germans—and the British if they join—would be sufficiently attracted by the idea of freer access to the American market to carry the more protectionist-minded French and Italians along with them.

The crucial question, however, is whether the United States Congress will give the Administration the new tariff-bargaining authority that the President has requested and that is necessary if the United States is to initiate a new drive for lower tariff barriers. The President has asked for general authority to reduce tariffs in reciprocal negotiations by fifty per cent, and special authority to negotiate elimination of tariffs on groups of products for which the United States and the European Economic Community between them account for more than eighty per cent or more of world trade in a representative period—the "dominant supplier" authority.

Both the sweeping nature of these powers and the emphasis on bargaining on a product-group basis would be new departures in American legislation, and are a response to the Common Market's procedures for moving towards internal free trade. To cushion the impact of loss of protection on American industry, the proposed legislation contains important and novel provisions for adjustment assistance to the industries and workers adversely affected, provisions which are the American parallel of aspects of the Rome Treaty that I have discussed.

In attempting to obtain power to initiate a new move towards freer trade at this time, the Administration faces considerable difficulty, because the higher average unemployment and the balance-of-payments deficits of the past four years have strengthened the arguments of the advocates of protection, just as the same phenomena have done in Canada. The proposed legislation attempts to meet these arguments both by retaining escape clauses and procedures and by providing adjustment assistance; and the "dominant supplier" authority is artfully framed to support the argument that the United States will gain from mutual tariff reduction under it, since the product groups included are those in which the United States has demonstrated superior competitive efficiency and flexibility. The case for the legislation is being presented to the American public not only as a help to the balance-of-payments but also as a challenge to the ability of the American enterprise system to compete in a free market; and it is conceivable that the Americans will rise to the challenge as the Europeans have done. It is certainly too early to write the new legislation off as already doomed to failure in Congress.

On the other hand, the continuance of the United States balance-of-payments deficit offers some ground for more general anxiety about the capacity of the United States to sustain leadership in the free world. The maintenance of a fixed exchange rate requires a country to pursue appropriate domestic policies, and may involve it in a conflict between balance-of-payments equilibrium on the one hand and domestic growth and full employment on the other. This problem has been plaguing the United States in recent years, and there has been some tendency to sacrifice growth and employment (not to speak of the niceties of liberal trade policy) to the balance of payments. So far the new Administration has not had to face this problem in an acute form—it was lucky enough to come into office near the bottom of a recession—but as the recovery proceeds the balance of payments may well deteriorate sharply, and the Administration be forced to choose between internal and external stability. If so, it is greatly to be hoped that it will choose to alter or abandon the present fixed rate of the dollar on gold rather than retreat into economic isolationism or deflationary policies.

## 6. STAGNATION IN
## THE CANADIAN ECONOMY,
## 1958-61

I HAVE ALREADY referred briefly to the growth boom that Canada and the United States enjoyed in the dozen years after the war, a boom based on increasingly close integration of the two economies through the process of investment of American capital in the production of

Canadian resource products for export to the American market, and to the decline in the rate of growth and increase in average unemployment in the subsequent four years. The more rapid growth of the Canadian than the American economy in the boom supported the development of an ebullient national confidence, and revived the sentiment that "the twentieth century belongs to Canada." At the same time the increasing interdependence between Canada and the United States, especially the high proportions of American goods in Canadian imports and of American capital in Canadian enterprises, prompted growing fears of "American domination" of Canada which expressed themselves in advocacy both of increased protection—a policy especially favoured by the representatives of Canadian subsidiaries of American firms— and of resort to Canada's traditional offset to the economic pull of the United States, a strengthening of Canada's trading relations with Britain. The virtual stagnation of the Canadian economy in the past four years has, so far as one can judge, sadly damaged Canadian confidence in the future. Slow growth and unemployment have strengthened anti-American sentiment and provided new arguments for protection, to which the Government has been giving legislative effect. European and Japanese competition in the Canadian market has increased the difficulties of Canadian manufacturers, and added a new and poignant note to their pleas for increased protection. The formation of the Common Market has faced Canada with a threat to her exports to Europe, and, unkindest cut of all, Britain's decision to apply for membership in the Common Market has kicked the props out from under the vague—and completely unimplemented—promise of the present Government to reduce Canada's economic dependence on the United States by diverting her trade towards the United Kingdom. Finally, President Kennedy's appeal to Congress for the new legislation required for a new American initiative towards freer trade has challenged Canada to declare her attitude on the future direction the system of international trade should take—a challenge to which the Canadian response has been characteristically conservative.

The changes in the world economy that I described earlier have in fact manifested themselves in two major problems. One has been the prolonged stagnation of the Canadian economy; the other, the direction Canadian trade policy should take in face of increasing foreign competition and the emergence of the Common Market. Of these the second has aroused the more public discussion. But the first is by far the more important, economically speaking; it is also a problem whose solution is fully within the competence of the Canadian government, unrestricted by dependence on the reactions of other countries' policies. I need scarcely point out that in dealing with neither of these problems has the record of the Canadian government been one of noticeably positive accomplishment.

When I speak of the virtual stagnation of the Canadian economy in the past four years, I am of course using a rather emotive term to describe some complex phenomena; and in saying that the remedy for stagnation is within the competence of the government, I do not wish to imply that all of these phenomena are equally tractable to government policy, or that there are no limits to what the government can do. Nor do I mean to imply that these phenomena appeared suddenly on January 1, 1958, without having made their presence known beforehand— economic history does not work that way. Nevertheless, there is a sharp enough difference between the economic condition of Canada in the past four years and in the preceding period to justify the descriptive term I have used; and the most important element of difference—unemployment—is well within the powers of government to handle.

I have already identified stagnation with slow growth and high average unemployment. As to unemployment, there can be no doubt of the difference between the past four years and the previous period, as the following statistics indicate: unemployment in Canada averaged 3 per cent in the four years 1950–53, and 4¼ per cent in the four years 1954–57, an average of 3.6 per cent over the first eight years of the 1950's; in the four years 1958–61, unemployment has averaged 6.8 per cent and in the past two years it has been over 7 per cent. As to growth, the statistics show a much less sharp change in the past four years as compared with previous experience, indicating instead a major change early in the 1950's: real gross national product per head of population grew at the compound rate of 3.28 per cent from the fourth quarter of 1948 to the second quarter of 1953, at the very much lower rate of .72 per cent from the second quarter of 1953 to the second quarter of 1957, and has actually declined since. Gross national product per head is a poor indicator of growth, however, since it absorbs the effects of changes in population structure, labour force participation rates, and unemployment. A better though still imperfect measure is gross national product per head of employed population: this grew at 4.02 per cent compounded and at 1.30 per cent compounded in the first two periods I mentioned, and at the still lower rate of .93 per cent compounded between the second quarter of 1957 and the first quarter of 1960, the last period for which I have official statistics.

Heavy unemployment and slow growth of productivity can both be regarded as evidence of stagnation, but they represent stagnation of different types, since they differ in their causation and amenability to governmental policy and in the appropriate remedy they call for. Let me consider them in turn.

## 7. THE UNEMPLOYMENT PROBLEM

HEAVY UNEMPLOYMENT, as Keynes taught (and some economists seem to have forgotten), is the consequence of inadequate demand for labour, and can be remedied by governmental policies designed to expand effective demand. In an open economy—one engaging in international trade—expansion of effective demand affects the current account of the balance of payments adversely, by increasing the demand for imports and possibly by reducing the supply of exports; in addition, and particularly if demand is expanded by reducing interest rates, the capital account of the balance of payments will be affected adversely by a tendency for people to borrow in the country and invest their savings elsewhere. In a country on a fixed exchange rate, the worsening of the balance of payments may result in a loss of reserves serious enough to threaten the stability of the exchange rate, and this consideration may force the government to stop expanding effective demand before unemployment is reduced to a satisfactorily low level—the problem that has plagued the United States in recent years. If, however, a country has a floating exchange, as Canada has had since 1950, the worsening of the balance of payments is automatically corrected by a depreciation of the exchange rate, and there is no external limit on the pursuit of a policy of maintaining high employment; the only limits are internal limits, arising from the fact that a lower percentage of unemployment is likely to be accompanied by a faster rate of price increase, and set by the relative weights the government policy-makers place on the disadvantages of higher unemployment as compared with a more rapid rate of price increase.

Now suppose a country with a floating exchange rate that has enjoyed a high level of employment accompanied by a noticeably rising trend of prices, and suppose that a variety of developments—a reduction in the rate of growth of demand for exports, increased competition from imports, a slackening of demand in the home market—reduces the level of demand for the country's output at the prevailing exchange rate and level of interest rates. The appropriate policy will obviously be an expansion of demand; and, if sustained growth is one of the government's objectives, the most appropriate way to expand demand will be by increasing the quantity of money and reducing interest rates. But suppose that the central bank instead chooses to follow a tight money policy, either because, being a central bank, it regards the preservation of the value of money as a moral issue, or because it is influenced by the fact that the other central banks in the world, which unlike itself are on fixed exchange rates and are trying to operate a fixed exchange rate system with inadequate reserves so that they have to be concerned with the influence of their domestic price levels on their international competitive position, have begun to lecture each other on the perils of inflation and the necessity of stopping it.

The result will be heavy unemployment in the country concerned, unemployment created either directly by the effect of tight money on the willingness of industry to invest, or indirectly by the effect of tight money on the exchange rate and the international competitive position of industry. The high exchange rate will lead industry to blame its difficulties on foreign competition and demand more protection; the more progressive business men will blame their troubles on low productivity, discover that to increase productivity costs more than it yields or requires concentration and rationalization of the country's industrial structure, and demand subsidies for new investment and research or relief from the restrictions the combines laws place on their freedom to divide up the market more profitably among them. The effect of high interest rates in inducing domestic enterprises and local governments to borrow abroad, and making domestic assets cheap for foreigners to acquire, will make it plausible to blame the high exchange rate and the resulting unemployment on foreign investment in the country. The reduction in government revenue resulting from lower incomes will unbalance the budget—which will prevent income and employment from sagging as badly as they otherwise would—and the government's need to borrow on a large scale to meet its deficits will make it plausible to blame the finance minister and not the central bank for high interest rates. Since a decline in demand is never spread evenly over the different industries, and since recent investment will have been undertaken in the expectation that the economy would continue to grow at its accustomed rate, it will be plausible to argue that unemployment is due to structural maladjustments of the economy and the errors of past investment decisions. Since skilled and educated employees are both more worth retention on a standby basis to their employers and more adaptable to alternative occupations, unemployment will be concentrated on the unskilled and the illiterate, and it will be plausible to argue that unemployment is due to insufficient education of the population. Since firms are likely to hold on to labour made redundant by labour-saving improvements when the labour market is tight and to discharge it when the labour market is easy, it will be plausible to attribute unemployment to labour-saving inventions and automation. It will also appear plausible to argue, quite fallaciously, that because firms are employing excess labour for the reasons just given an expansion of demand will not increase employment, when the correct inference is, of course, that demand needs to be expanded more than would appear necessary at first sight. Thus all sorts of explanations of unemployment will be advanced other than the fundamental one, the inappropriate monetary policy of the central bank, and memories being short and unemployment easy for the employed to get used to and rationalize, the central bank will even be congratulated for its firmness in resisting inflation; and it will become a matter of boastful pride whenever unemployment falls to a level considerably higher than used to prevail.

This theoretical analysis seems to me to fit fairly closely to what has been going on in the Canadian economy in recent years, at least until the change in fiscal policy and replacement of the Governor of the Bank of Canada in mid-1961. Regardless of the details of the explanation, it is certain that the shift from a 4¼ per cent to a 6.8 per cent level of unemployment has cost Canada a great deal in foregone production and real income, not to speak of the social costs and misery of unemployment, which have fallen particularly hard on the young and the immigrant.

Just how great the cost has been is a difficult matter to estimate, but it is considerably greater than the unemployment figures alone would indicate. This is because an increase in unemployment is accompanied by a reduction in the hours worked by those remaining employed and a decrease in their productivity, and by a reduction in the numbers in the labour force. In the United States, the Council of Economic Advisers has calculated[1] that a one point reduction in the percentage of unemployment towards four per cent is accompanied by a three per cent increase in gross national product. If this calculation is anywhere near applicable to Canada, it would indicate that the difference between the seven per cent average unemployment of 1960 and 1961 and the 4¼ per cent average of 1954–57 corresponded to a loss of gross national product of between two and a half and three billion dollars in each of the last two years. It is that sort of order of magnitude, in comparison with other estimates of the cost to Canada of the new trading arrangements in Europe to which I shall refer later, that underlies my judgment that the problem of stagnation is far more serious for Canada than the problem of trade policy.

As I pointed out at the start of my theoretical argument, there is no external restraint on the pursuit of a full employment policy in a country with a floating rate of exchange. The only restraint in principle is the economic cost of the inflationary trend of prices generally associated with levels of unemployment. A great deal has been written and said about the costs and dangers of inflation in North America in the past five years: but

[1]*Economic Report of the President.* Transmitted to the Congress, Jan. 1962. Together with the *Annual Report of the Council of Economic Advisers* (Washington: US Government Printing Office, 1962), pp. 49–53, esp. p. 50.

most of it has had no basis in fact whatsoever. Nor has any serious attempt been made to calculate the magnitude of the alleged economic cost of the kind of inflation in question, and compare it with the cost of unemployment. To begin with, there is good reason to question how much genuine inflation there has been: consumer price indexes are well known to contain a significant upward bias, owing to the fact that new goods are not included until most of the reduction in their cost made possible by mass production has already occurred, and that insufficient account is taken of improvements in the quality of goods, especially durable goods. A group of economists who studied the rise in the American consumer price index between 1953 and 1960—which rise was roughly the same as the rise in the Canadian price index—concluded that the rise could be accounted for entirely by quality improvements, and that the true index had not risen and might have fallen in the period.[2] Second, there is reason to doubt that the price index, especially in an open economy, is very sensitive to changes in unemployment: the Canadian consumer price index, for example, rose at the rate of 1.6 per cent per annum from 1953 to 1958 and at the rate of 1.1 per cent per annum from 1958 to 1961—a reduction of .5 percentage points in the rate of increase associated with (not even necessarily caused by) the substantial change in average unemployment I have already described. Third, and most important, the evidence does not sup-

[2]The research on which the conclusion is based may be found in *Government Price Statistics*. Hearings before the Subcommittee on Economic Statistics of the Joint Economic Committee, Congress of the United States, 87th Cong., 1st sess., Part I, Jan. 24, 1961. The inclusion referred to was given to me as the consensus of the economists by Professor George J. Stigler, Chairman of the Research Committee.

port the usual myths about inflation: that wages lag behind prices, that inflation causes massive redistributions of income, that inflation distorts and hinders the functioning of a competitive economy, that inflation reduces savings and economic growth, that inflation inevitably accelerates into hyperinflation, that inflation— or even hyperinflation—inevitably leads to monetary collapse. The fundamental reason why all these allegations about inflation turn out to be myths is that income-earners and investors quickly get used to continuing inflation, and their recognition of it is expressed in a compensating increase in money rates of interest; consequently the main effect of inflation is the minor inefficiency resulting from the fact that higher rates of interest induce people to economize on the use of money at a cost in real resources. I should perhaps emphasize that I am speaking here of continuing inflation in a peace-time free enterprise economy, not of inflation suddenly imposed on an economy by the needs of wartime finance and accompanied by price and income controls—a much more demonstrably evil type of inflation, which the central banks of North America did nothing to prevent when it happened.

I have so far been arguing that the unemployment that has characterized the Canadian economy for the past four years has been a direct consequence of Canadian government policy (or lack of policy) and specifically of the policy of the central bank; and I have argued that the only reasonable justification for this policy—the necessity of stopping inflation—has been an extremely weak one when evaluated by its extremely tenuous economic benefits and serious economic consequences. I do not wish to imply that none of the factors to which others have pointed in explanation have played any part—

obviously adjustment to the slowing down of growth in the United States and the emergence of Europe as an international competitor would have imposed strains on the Canadian industrial structure under even the most favourable economic conditions—but I would argue strongly that these strains would have been far more easily absorbed by the normal processes of competitive adjustment in a mature industrial economy had activity and employment been maintained at high levels.

Before I leave this subject, let me make two brief observations on some more general aspects of the difficulties Canada has had with its central bank in the past four years. The first is that these difficulties amply demonstrate that, to ensure the efficient conduct of monetary policy, it is not enough to select intelligent, responsible, and well-trained people and put them in charge of the central bank's policy operations armed only with general instructions to aim at some vaguely described desirable general objectives. Without concrete specification of the objectives to be aimed at and a clear understanding of the procedures to be followed in achieving them, it is only too easy for the central bank to cover up its mistakes or disguise the fact that it is pursuing other objectives than those intended, and only too difficult for outside observers to detect these mistakes or covert changes in objective. This problem has appeared at various times since the war in each of the three countries I know well; in the United States it has led a number of economists to propose a reform that I think deserves serious consideration: that the central bank should be bound to follow some simple rule of monetary management, for example to increase the money supply at a constant rate corresponding to the long-run rate of growth of the need for money at a stable price level, this rule to be based on economic research into the relation of money to the functioning of the economy. Such a rule would not necessarily be absolutely binding or unchangeable; but it would provide a standard of reference by which to judge the performance of the central bank superior to the present practice of judging central banks largely by the persuasiveness of their own descriptions of what they are doing.

My second observation is that the recent fracas over monetary policy in Canada suggests that some of the traditions that Canada has taken over from Britain may be inappropriate to the efficient conduct of policy. One of these clearly is the tradition of central bank independence, transferred to Canada in the 1930's when it was thought that the achievement of dominion status required a country to establish its own imitation of the Bank of England; in my judgment, the traditional independence of the Bank of England has been a behind-the-scenes source of trouble for the economic policy of the United Kingdom itself. Another possibly inappropriate tradition is the tradition of the career civil service, at least as it affects the top echelons. A civil service, particularly when one party is in power for a long time, develops its own views of what policy should be, and this makes it difficult for a new government to take over with the assurance that the new policies it wants will be put into operation. Observation of the ferment of ideas now going on in Washington suggests that the freedom allowed by the flexibility of the American system to bring fresh minds to bear directly on policy problems has much to recommend it, as compared with the dependence on royal commissions that the Canadian system of government entails.

## 8. THE PROBLEM OF GROWTH

LET ME NOW turn to the second aspect of stagnation, the slow growth of productivity. On this subject economic theory has much less to say, because the central problem involves the determinants of the rates at which economic variables change, and economic theory has until very recently been mostly concerned with the determinants of the direction of change of economic variables rather than the speed of change.

I have already mentioned one way by which the rate of growth of productivity could be increased—by raising the level of demand and reducing unemployment. This method hinges on the fact that when economic conditions are depressed improvements in methods of production occur that are not fully reflected in increases in measured productivity because firms are operating below capacity, but that will be exploited as the economy moves to a higher level of activity. The presence of such latent increases in productivity reflects the more fundamental principle that unless demand is increased sufficiently to absorb the additional output that technical progress and capital investment make possible, the fruits of such improvements in productive potential will appear in the form of productivity increases only to the extent that they also appear in the form of increased unemployment. Thus policies designed to increase productivity must be complemented by policies designed to increase effective demand correspondingly if they are to be effective in increasing output—a point frequently overlooked by those who stress increased productivity as the solution to depression and unemployment.

The increase in productivity that accompanies increased economic activity, however, can provide only a transient increase in the rates of growth of productivity—though it is not, of course, to be despised on that account. The more difficult problem for policy is how to increase the normal rate of increase of productivity, say, the rate of increase of productivity the economy would enjoy at a given percentage of unemployment constant over time. The difficulties of this problem are inherent in three subtleties that are generally overlooked by those with easy answers: first, mathematically a rate of increase has both a numerator and a denominator; second, by assumption the available resources of the economy at any one time are given; third, policy cannot operate directly on productivity itself but must operate on the factors that determine productivity.

One might suppose, for example, that full employment, as contrasted with high average unemployment, would stimulate the rate of productivity increase by providing a combination of buoyant demand and a tight labour market. But while such conditions will tend to increase the absolute amount of productivity-increasing investment and research, they will not necessarily have enough effect to make the larger income of a full-employment economy grow faster than the smaller income of a less fully employed economy. In fact, comparative evidence shows no close association between a country's rate of economic growth and its unemployment percentage. Similarly, a more sophisticated theoretical analysis might lead one to suppose that a country's rate of growth will be higher, the higher the proportion of its income it saves and invests. This is in fact a basic proposition in the modern theory of economic growth; and it must be true provided that investment is as productive in high-saving as in low-saving countries. But there is nothing to prevent a high rate of saving from being offset by a low productivity-increasing effect of investment; and in fact historical and comparative evidence shows no close relation between saving ratios and growth rates. The same qualification applies to the proposition that a country's rate of growth will be higher the more, proportionately, it spends on research; and while I have no figures on the matter, I strongly suspect that this proposition would be as hard to verify as the corresponding proposition about investment. I must add, however, for purposes of later argument, that these remarks do not in any way deny the possibility, indeed probability, that by raising its proportionate expenditure on investment or research a country can increase its growth rate temporarily; the question is rather how long it would be before the stimulus to growth from a higher savings ratio was offset by the need to resort to low productivity-increasing investment or research to dispose of the extra expenditure.

In spite of the theoretical difficulties I have outlined, the growth-accelerating potential of new investment and scientific research has so captured the imagination of influential opinion, including that of some economists, in Canada and elsewhere that it has been widely recommended that government should subsidize investment and research expenditure by tax concessions; and these recommendations have been or may be given legislative effect. Attractive as this device may seem at first sight, economic theory suggests that such subsidies are likely to reduce growth rather than increase it: there is no convincing reason for believing that the forms of expenditure chosen for such favour yield a return to the economy as a whole significantly in excess of the private return that the firms undertaking the expenditure would normally consider—the only theoretical justification for a subsidy on specific forms of investment expenditure—and the resulting insertion of consideration of possible tax advantages into the firm's calculations of the profitability of such expenditures is likely to distort the allocation of investment funds and reduce the average return on investment to the economy as a whole. It may be objected that these subsidies will increase total investment. But, barring the possibility of a high interest-elasticity of supply of saving, this could only occur if either there are unemployed resources which can become employed in the additional investment (a possibility I have ruled out by assuming a given percentage of unemployment) or the government makes more resources available by increasing taxes or reducing expenditure; and in either case it is likely that the additional resources would be much more efficiently allocated among alternative productivity-increasing forms of expenditure by a general reduction in interest rates than by a system of tax concessions on specific items of productivity-increasing expenditure.

To put the same argument in a more positive form: if it is desired to increase the rate of growth of an economy operating at a normal level of unemployment, the first requirement is to increase the rate of saving by budgetary means; if that is done, there is a strong case for leaving the allocation of savings among alternative investment and research opportunities to the normal competitive processes of the market, rather than trying to direct this allocation by the crude and unreliable device of tax concessions. In choosing, say, research expenditure for special tax favour, the government has no way of knowing whether research expenditure increases productivity more than would, say, the availability of cheaper credit to unincorporated businesses; and it is quite possible that the tax favours will encourage research that has no effect in increasing productivity or even reduces it. Whether an increase in savings squeezed out of the economy by fiscal means and passed back into it by lowering interest rates would produce a substantial and sustained increase in the growth rate is another question; there may be some significance in the fact that the period of most rapid North American economic growth—immediately after the war—was characterized by budget surpluses and low interest rates, while the subsequent period of slower growth has been characterized by budget deficits and higher interest rates.

In presenting the foregoing arguments, I have assumed the desirability of a more rapid rate of growth, and have concerned myself with the question of how economic policy might set about achieving it. It has become customary in modern discussions of economic policy to attach considerable importance to the rate of economic growth, and to identify virtuous and successful economic management with the achievement of a high rate of economic growth. Much of this emphasis on growth, however, is a by-product of the cold war and the rivalry of the United States with Russia for the political support of the underdeveloped countries—and, in Canada, of rivalry with the United States. It can be argued that on strictly economic grounds there is little reason for a government in a mature industrial society based on free enterprise principles to make economic growth for its own sake an object of policy and that—provided full employment is maintained—the rate of growth should be left to be determined by private decisions about saving and investment. This argument, however, ignores completely the large role that government plays in a modern economy, and the fact that the presence of government as a taxer and spender and as a major debtor tends by itself to reduce the rate of economic growth below the socially optimal rate. The size of the government's budgetary operations inevitably makes it an influence on the rate of growth, through the influence of the government's surplus or deficit on the supply of saving available for private investment. Further, the presence of a large public debt, by providing the public with a supply of assets to which there corresponds no equivalent stock of real capital, tends to reduce the desire to save; what is probably much more important, the financing of governmental activities by taxation of income makes the marginal private return to investment significantly lower than the marginal social return, thereby making the rate of saving and investment lower than it would be if savers received the full social return on their investment. There is, therefore, a *prima facie* case, on strictly economic grounds, for the government to stimulate economic growth by increasing the rate of saving in the economy by budgeting for a surplus, and ensuring that the saving is translated into investment by pursuing an appropriately easy monetary policy.

## 9. THE PROBLEM OF
## FOREIGN TRADE POLICY

I HAVE DWELT rather extensively on the domestic problem of economic stagnation, because I consider it by far the more important of the two problems in which the changing nature of the world economy has manifested itself in

Canada, and also much more within the control of the Canadian Government's economic policy. Let me now turn to the other problem, the problem of the direction Canadian trade policy should take in face of the growth of international competition in manufacturing and the emergence of the Common Market. Public discussion of this problem in Canada has been mostly concerned with the implications of the emergence of the Common Market as the largest protected trading area in the world, and has focused on the dilemma the Common Market poses—especially if Britain joins—for the two traditional bases of Canadian commercial policy, reliance on trade with Europe to offset the economic pull of the United States, and reliance on protection of secondary manufacturing to promote Canadian industrial growth in rivalry with the United States. The dilemma is that the Common Market, especially if it includes Britain, threatens to restrict Canada's exports to Europe; but that any effort to prevent or offset the threatened restriction of European imports from Canada by new trade arrangements will require a lowering or elimination of Canada's protective tariffs. Faced with this dilemma, the Canadian Government has devoted its efforts to a vain—in both senses of the word—and undignified effort to deter the British from seeking or gaining membership in the Common Market, while denying the feasibility or desirability of any of the alternative trading arrangements that its critics have with more or less enthusiasm been recommending. The adoption of this posture inevitably calls to mind a cartoon by David Low which appeared sometime during the war: the cartoon depicts Colonel Blimp in the steam room of his club, proclaiming with great emphasis "By gad, sir, what we have we'll hold—if we can get it back!" The new developments in international relations obviously call for a more positive policy than this; and Canadians have not been backward in putting forward suggestions for new departures in Canadian commercial policy.

Before I discuss alternative possible policies, I must point out that the adverse effects on Canada's economic welfare and growth of the formation of the Common Market and Britain's impending adhesion to it have been greatly exaggerated in recent Canadian discussion and policy, and that the problem is of far less economic significance than the domestic problem of stagnation. Popular discussion tends universally to exaggerate the influence of other countries' commercial policies on a country's economic welfare, mainly because in assessing the effects of tariff changes people—even trained economists who ought to know better—fall back on the weak analytical instrument of political imagination rather than the scientific tools of economic analysis. Thus it is commonly assumed that loss of a preference or an increase in the duty levied in a foreign market will wipe out all trade and leave the resources that produce the goods concerned entirely unemployed. This assumption may be valid for considering the immediate effect of a sudden and unexpected loss of preference or tariff increase on an inflexible economy that does not pursue a full employment policy and maintains a rigid exchange rate; but it is certainly invalid for considering the effect of a change in tariffs that is phased over a period of years and well publicized in advance, on an economy that is reasonably flexible and sensibly managed. In such an economy—and the Canadian economy is reasonably flexible, and could be sensibly managed—one would expect the resources employed in producing the affected exports to shift to producing for other markets, or, if they could not so shift, to accept the relative lowering of their real incomes necessary to enable them to continue to dispose of their products in their accustomed markets.

Also, one would expect that, once the adjustments to the higher trade barriers had been made, the affected country's exports to the tariff-raising country would tend to grow along with any expansion in that country's total income—contrary to the popular notion that a tariff barrier around a market cuts the outside world off from participation in the growth of that market. Thus the loss inflicted by the raising of tariffs against a country's exports would be a once-over loss, whose annual magnitude would be determined by the flexibility of the economy affected, the extent to which tariffs were raised against it, and the amount of trade subject to those tariffs. "The flexibility of the economy" is a portmanteau term for the degree to which the economy can escape the necessity of accepting lower incomes by shifting its resources to alternative uses, and is extremely difficult if not impossible to quantify. But the other two determinants of the annual loss are quantifiable, and permit one to estimate, at least roughly, the magnitude of the maximum annual loss that a country may suffer from an increase in the tariffs it faces. That maximum loss is the decrease in the average price of its exports that would be necessary to offset the increase in the average tariff rate facing them, multiplied by the quantity of exports in question.

This method of estimation has been applied by Dr. Grant Reuber[3] to estimate the maximum cost to Canada of the increases in tariffs on exports of Canadian industrial materials to Europe—over half of Canada's total

[3]G. L. Reuber, "Western Europe's Demand for Canadian Industrial Materials," *Canadian Journal of Economics and Political Science*, XXVIII, no. 1 (Feb., 1962), pp. 16–34, esp. Table VI, p. 32.

exports to Europe—that would follow the establishment of a Common Market including Britain and the Six, on the extreme assumption that the price reductions required to offset increased tariffs would have to be granted to all Canada's other customers. Dr. Reuber arrives at a figure of $157 million (.45 per cent of gross national product) as the maximum cost estimate for 1959 trade; of this $157 million, $64 million represents the extra cost imposed by British membership in the Common Market. No estimate has been made (or could yet be made) of the cost to Canada of the Common Market's common agricultural protective policy and of Britain's participation in it; but detailed studies of the competitive position of Canadian agriculture in Europe and consideration of the likely development of European agricultural policy do not suggest that the loss will be great. Dr. S. F. Kaliski[4] has attempted a comprehensive estimate of the annual cost to Canada of the loss of preferences in the British market, and arrived at an outside limit of $55 million. Both Reuber's and Kaliski's estimates are rough and incomplete, but at least they give some idea of the orders of magnitude of the loss to Canada involved in the establishment of the Common Market and British membership in it. The estimated maximum costs are not insubstantial, especially for the individual industries on which the tariff changes concerned would bear most heavily; but when placed alongside the estimated loss from unemployment of $2½ to $3 billion that I mentioned earlier, or Professor J. H. Young's well-known estimate of $1 billion as the cost of protection to the Canadian consumer,[5] they suggest very clearly that the alarm that has been

[4]S. F. Kaliski, "Canada, the United Kingdom and the Common Market," *International Journal*, XVII, no. 1 (winter, 1961–62) pp. 17–24, esp. p. 21.

[5]J. H. Young, *Canadian Commercial Policy* (Ottawa: Royal Commission on Canada's Economic Prospects, 1958), chap. VI, p. 73.

generated by the Common Market, and especially by Britain's desire to join it, has not been justified by a corresponding importance of these new developments in Europe's trading relationships to the Canadian standard of living. I would emphasize that these estimates are maximum estimates, and that the real loss is likely to be much less than the figures I have given; and that the estimates take no account of the indirect benefits to Canada that would result if, as the British believe, membership in the Common Market assisted Britain to solve its chronic balance-of-payments problem and accelerate its rate of economic growth.

## 10. CHOICES IN CANADA'S COMMERCIAL POLICY

THE ANALYSIS I have just presented is intended to place the adverse effects of the Common Market on Canadian trade in their proper economic perspective. I now turn to consider the chief proposals that have been made for change in Canada's commercial policy in face of the new developments in international trading relationships. Given the character of the Common Market as a novel and exciting scheme for achieving reciprocal free trade in a large market on a regional basis, and the traditional concentration of Canadian trading interests on the two areas of Europe and the United States, it is natural that these proposals have taken the form of advocacy of a similar regional grouping in which Canada would be included. But most such proposals have shown little understanding of either the political motivation of the European Economic Community or of what is involved in the formation of a customs union or common market. I shall ignore the more far-fetched of these proposals, and in discussing the major ones will draw summarily on various arguments and considerations that are implicit in my earlier account of the postwar evolution of the world economy.

The emergence of the Common Market as a rival trading bloc to the United States and the spectacle of Europe's rapid economic growth have prompted the proposal that Canada should join the European Economic Community, or seek associate membership in it, a proposal which has the appeal of conformity with the traditional Canadian policy of relying on trade with Europe to offset the economic pull of the United States. This proposal, however, ignores both the ultimate political objective of political union of Europe that underlies the Common Market, an objective that allows no place for Canada as a non-European country, and the prerequisites for successful economic union specified in the philosophy of the Common Market, prerequisites that past Canadian economic relations with Europe do not fulfil. It is simply not open to Canada to join the Common Market. Nor is it at all likely that Canada could obtain association with the Common Market: while the article of the Rome Treaty pertaining to association of other countries with the Common Market technically would permit some sort of Canadian association, it is clear that the article was included for the benefit of other European countries and of colonies achieving nationhood, not of countries like Canada. Quite apart from the fact that Canada does not belong with Europe and would be unlikely to be welcome in it, it is extremely doubtful that a mutually satisfactory form of association could be worked out that would pass the GATT rules against discriminatory trading arrangements, especially as the United States' willingness to support the Common Market in the interests of strengthening Europe economically and politically would be unlikely to extend to tolerance of such an arrangement. Finally, it is *prima facie* likely that Canada would lose rather than gain economically from a trade relationship with Europe that discriminated sharply against the United States. The reason is that the elimination of Canadian tariffs on imports of manufactures from Europe, while it would lead to replacement of high-cost Canadian manufactures by lower-cost European manufactures, would also divert Canadian imports from lower-cost United States sources to higher-cost European sources, and since the United States provides such a large share of Canadian imports the potential loss from trade diversion could easily be substantial.

Appreciation of the potential economic cost to Canada of an economic union with Europe and unwillingness to sacrifice Canada's political and economic ties with the United States have prompted the alternative suggestion of an Atlantic Economic Community embracing Europe, the United States, and Canada. This scheme has the appeal of protecting both of Canada's major trading interests simultaneously; but it has two major drawbacks. One is that it is unlikely to attract the Europeans, to whom the erection of a common tariff barrier is an economic prerequisite of European unification; the other is that it would conflict with important United States commitments to and political interests in Latin America, Asia, and Africa. The North Atlantic Economic

Community would be a rich man's club and a white
man's club, and even if it devoted a larger proportion of
its riches to carrying the white man's burden its existence
would be highly unpopular in the rest of the non-communist world, especially if its major motivation appeared
to be to support an aggressively anti-communist military
alliance. Attempts have been made to give it a broader
cultural and political justification by appealing to the
notion of a "North Atlantic Community" of nations with
common institutions, history, and ideals; but this notion
has all the earmarks of a dangerous political fiction—
dangerous because it usually comes into play as part of
an endeavour to secure for the country in which it is
advanced a position of political importance enjoyed in
an earlier period but no longer consistent with economic
and political facts. Thus in the United States the notion
of the "Atlantic Community" is advanced in the hope of
persuading the Europeans to assume without qualification the objectives of United States foreign policy; in
Canada it is advanced in the hope of restoring Canada's
war and postwar roles as mediator between the United
States and the United Kingdom and spokesman for the
new nations; in England it is advanced in the hope of
restoring the United Kingdom's "special relationship"
among European countries with the United States—all of
which ambitions have been rendered anachronistic by the
shift in the balance of economic power towards continental Europe, an area where the notion of Atlantic
Community seems to generate little enthusiasm except
among militant anti-communists.

A third alternative is the proposal for a customs union,
a free trade area, or "selective" free trade between
Canada and the United States, a proposal prompted by
recognition of the extent to which the North American

economies have become economically integrated in the postwar period, and by the desire to increase the efficiency of the Canadian economy by exposing Canadian producers to the free play of competition and securing for them the ready access to a large market required for the exploitation of economies of mass production and modern technology. This proposal, in contrast with the others, contains all the ingredients usually thought necessary for successful economic integration— territorial contiguity, similarity of social, economic, and cultural characteristics, and a long history of close economic collaboration—as well as the potentiality of a substantial net gain in economic efficiency, according to the economic theory of customs unions. The main objection to this proposal is, as it always has been, political rather than economic, derived from the fear of political absorption of Canada by the United States. That fear seems to me completey irrational, an anachronism inherited from a historical era that has long since passed away. In the nineteenth century, when economic development in North America was based on the settlement and exploitation of new farming regions and when the United States was bent on territorial expansion, there was good reason for that fear. In the twentieth century, economic development is no longer based on land settlement— indeed, like most other advanced nations, Canada and the United States suffer from an embarrassing surplus of farmers—and the United States has long since ceased to seek expansion by the acquisition of new territory. In fact, a Canadian demand to join the United States would be acutely embarrassing to the United States, as political union with Canada would wreck the delicate political balance that the United States has worked out between the North and South and between the industrial and farming groups.

But the occasion for a deliberate policy of seeking economic integration with the United States is not available now, and may never occur. Such an endeavour would represent the acceptance by Canada and the United States of the trend towards regionalization of world trade, and the American Administration is instead seeking to contain that trend in a new movement towards non-discriminatory multilateral free trade. I would strongly suggest that Canada's economic interests lie in the same direction, and that Canada should support to the full the new American initiative by declaring her willingness to reduce or eliminate tariffs, reserving the possibility of North American regional integration for subsequent exploration in the event that the United States initiative should fail to win acceptance by the United States Congress or—the other hurdle that has to be crossed—by the European Economic Community.

My reasons for this recommendation follow from my earlier analysis of the spread of industrialization around the world and the requirements of sustained domestic economic progress in a changing world economy—flexibility in changing from activities in which comparative advantage is disappearing to activities in which new comparative advantage is appearing. The more liberal the trading policies pursued by other nations, the greater the opportunity for Canada to exploit its comparative advantages by developing to the full the advantages of large-scale production and technological leadership in specialized branches of economic activity. Much more important, the lower the level of Canadian tariffs, the greater the freedom of Canadian producers to determine where Canadian comparative advantage lies and to exploit it to the fullest possible extent.

Protection is generally advocated as a means of raising the standard of living and promoting economic growth.

In fact the reverse is the truth, at least in an advanced economy like Canada's. Protection promotes inefficient allocation of resources; in place of industrial specialization and the economies of large-scale production, it fosters fragmentation of the market, inefficiently small production units, excessive diversification of product, and short production runs. I have noticed, incidentally, that it has become fashionable to blame these phenomena of inefficiency—like all the rest of Canada's economic problems—on American investment in Canada; but the slightest observation of other small economies is sufficient to demonstrate that resort to protectionism can produce these and other examples of wasteful inefficiency without any American help whatsoever. By fostering inefficiency, the tariff reduces the standard of living; the cost of protection to the Canadian consumer, as I have mentioned, has been estimated at about one billion dollars per year, a figure that accounts for about one fifth of the difference between the Canadian standard of living and the American. What is more important in the long run, an established policy of protection promotes resistance to economic change, resistance that takes the form of demanding increased protection to avoid the need for adapting to change; but change—especially change in other countries—cannot be stopped by the tariff; all that increased protection can do is to waste resources in a futile effort to resist the irresistible.

But it is not sufficient, in the modern world, simply to rehearse the classical arguments for free trade. It is necessary to recognize and take account of the functions the tariff performs, and to substitute more efficient methods of performing these functions. In the first place, the tariff has been used to encourage investment in particular lines of production, investment that has been undertaken in the expectation of profits guaranteed by the tariff; the substitution of private for governmental decisions about the most profitable lines of investment entailed in removing tariff protection should logically be accompanied by compensation to the industries concerned for the loss of their profit opportunities. Secondly, and of more lasting importance, it should be recognized that the tariff has become an instrument for cushioning the impact of adverse economic changes on particular industries and regions. As a form of social security for unfortunate businesses and their employees the tariff has notorious defects; but failing alternative methods of assistance, there will inevitably be demands for tariff support. It is for this reason that the Treaty of Rome provides for a Social Fund and an Investment Bank, and President Kennedy's new tariff legislation provides for adjustment assistance. Adjustment assistance is a positive and constructive solution to the problem of helping industries adversely affected by foreign competition, far more so than tariff increases; I would suggest only that it should not be restricted to assisting adjustment to foreign competition, but should be designed to assist industries afflicted by the effects of rapid economic change whether that change is foreign or domestic. I would also point out that, with the international competition that low tariffs or free trade would encourage, it would no longer be necessary for the combines administration to keep a suspicious eye on co-operative efforts by Canadian industry to adjust to economic change.

I have been recommending the abandonment of Canada's traditional policy of promoting industrialization by tariff protection, in favour of a liberal trading policy better designed to foster Canadian growth in a changing world economy. Acceptance of this recommendation requires a fundamental rethinking of accepted ideas on Canada's place in the world economy, a rethinking that the changing shape of the world economy has made long overdue. Canadian economic policy has historically been dominated by the ambition to create a country rival in power to the United States, and so to prove that the Americans were wrong to revolt from colonial rule in 1776. The ambition to outgrow the United States is a futile one: in spite of the boasting about Canada's faster growth in the postwar period, it is a fact that that growth was insufficient to raise the ratio of the Canadian to the American population to what it was in 1860. For the sake of interest, I calculated the date at which Canada's population would equal the population of the United States, if both countries' populations continued to grow at the 1949–60 rate. That happy event is due to occur, as near as I can reckon it, at 9.36 p.m. on the 22nd of January, 2212 A.D.—212 years after the end of the twentieth century that Sir Wilfrid Laurier claimed for Canada.

The ambition to surpass the United States is not only hopeless but pointless. It is quite clear that, if the twentieth century does not belong to Canada, it does not belong to the United States either: it belongs to all the nations of the world, according to their capacity to make the best of the resources they have. In that endeavour Canada has a fortunate head start over most nations of comparable size, in technology, capital, human skill and natural resources; and she has every chance of continued prosperity and growth provided she has the courage and wisdom to manage her economic affairs intelligently.